Copyright

Out of The Chrysalis: Your Catalyst

All rights reserved. No part of this publication may be reproduced, stored in a retrieval system, or transmitted in any form or by any means-electronic, mechanical, photocopy, recording or any other-except brief quotations in printed reviews, without prior permission of the publisher. Bible verses are taken from various translations of the Holy Bible.

Anointed Hands Publishing (Nina Motivates LLC)

www.ninamotivates.info

publishernina@gmail.com

Graphics and Marketing: Shawn Robinson

727 Marketing: www.727marketingllc.com

Copyright© 2021, by Tesia Watkins,

All rights reserved

ISBN: 978-1-7365910-1-7

This Book Belongs To

_____

Dedication

I dedicate this book to 03/28/22, age 25. Great things are in store according to the LORD.

Thank You

LORD, I am grateful to have my first book published.

Thank you, to my friends and family. Whether old, new, former, or current; you were an important part. Whatever part you played; I love you.

To my parents, thank you, specifically.

To myself, nice work!

And to my daughter, thank you for being Precious.

Table of Content

Disclaimer — 1

Introduction: Understanding 101 — 2

Lesson One: Love Freely — 4

Lesson Two: Know Your Friends — 13

Lesson Three: Accept the Truth Of Others And Prioritize Your Own — 23

Lesson Four: Apologize — 31

Lesson Five: Trust People to Be Themselves Not Who You Want Them to Be — 37

Lesson Six: Do Not Assume They Know — 43

Lesson Seven: Forgive — 49

Lesson Eight: Have Trust and Put It in God — 56

Lesson Nine: Value Patience and Those Who Are Patient with You — 63

Lesson Ten: Start Again and Keep Going — 67

Happy You Made It! — 69

Side Notes — 74

Meet the Author — 76

Disclaimer: This process works best if you are honest with where you are in your heart. You do not have to push your feelings away lightly; they are a nuisance. You process your feelings and work through them like you do with clothes. Clothes? Yes, you dress according to how you are feeling within the parameters of where you are going. You wash your clothes, fold them, hang them up, and get rid of the ones that no longer match you. These lessons are not to be taken and learned within your feelings but are to be parameters through which you grow into a liberated version of yourself. The writing of these lessons took deep reflection of who I am and things I have done. Even as I share the faults and turning points of my life with you, I want you to do the same with yourself. Nothing is one sided and those nameless figures I mention in my stories have their own perspective and reality. I write this to you free from ought, fear to love, and free from a self-created cage of self-preservation. Also, I will use capital LORD as an abbreviation for YHWH as they do in the KJV and bibles across the world.

See you on the other side!

Introduction: Understanding 101

Time is not the healer of all things but, in time hopefully, all things heal. Platonic friendships, romantic relationships, and even our own identity are out of the hands of time. Concerning these three topics, healing comes through tests and trials. Hopefully, this book gives you a boost in your healing process. Our healing lies within the lessons we have learned within our friendships. Lessons about people, ourselves, and the dynamic of the connection. We learn to set standards for what makes a person a good friend to us, as well as boundaries we should work to maintain. Healing for our romantic trials comes in balancing wisdom and hope. The wisdom that comes from love gained, lost, and returned, from being mishandled, giving forgiveness, and trying at love again. Lastly, the common denominator of both friendship and love, Self. You learn much about yourself in each dynamic. Learning yourself is not what brings healing to you, but it is the progression made from your less mature, most uninformed version of yourself in truth. In truth you are free from bitterness and using the compassion you had in those relationships.

Many people brag about keeping their guard up. None of them trust as they use to or love to the same capacity. These people are not living as free as they talk. So, let me challenge that mindset by stating the fact a guard is a burden. Let us drop our guards for a moment to produce boundaries. A boundary reminds you of your freedom. It is not something you wear on the outside, it establishes itself on the inside of you. The manifestation is in your words and actions combined. In other words, people know how far they can go comfortably and when they are close to provoking you to become offended or defensive. This method allows you to be yourself in any area. The atmosphere set will be the one you have established.

In these lessons, I have learned how to uphold my boundary without compromising who I have become over the years. Hopefully, you too will find the freedom to be you. First, let me say guards come in handy. They are there in case an enemy is close. It is not for us to walk through each day as if we are surrounded by our enemy or on guard and in fear of attack. So, consider this first rule as a foundation to healing the first thing that time does not heal... Identity.

Lesson One: Love Freely

We are not built to love only those who love us. Consider Matthew 5:47

We must love freely. You cannot keep hurt, resentment, despise, and hatred bottled up within your hearts. Everything you produce passes through your heart. If you write music, a post, text, or draw then that hesitation to love freely will be found in your words. I see bitter posts daily, with agreeing comments, likes, loves, and shares. The commenters are also hurt, and, in all actuality, it is hurt people telling each other how to patch up the wound rather than heal it. I have never been the type to say let it go. I believe "let it go" does not tell you how to do what it is saying to do. Instead, I say love through it.

Do not regret whomever you have shown kindness to or became vulnerable with when you were being yourself. Do not be apologetic for loving someone who others deemed unlovable or hard to tolerate. You are the best part of humanity when you are doing that. You have been wounded as a result of trying to love someone. Now adjust. Remember we are talking about Loving freely in the context of being yourself. I am talking to the person who has come to regret the way they do things.

Okay, Storytime... in high school I was friendly and all my life I have been a giver. There would be times that I would do something nice for someone else because of who I am, and they would misinterpret the action. Eventually, I would have to have some sort of awkward conversation explaining my actions were only a part of who I was and not because of romantic interest. Years later I entered a ministry consistent with who I am, I gave in time, in service, and more for my love of the LORD. Eventually, my motive was in question and I received a prophetic word publicly saying that I am genuine. This word vindicated me. I knew that I was doing from the heart but, being in question made me not want to continue how I have always been. I did not want to help clean because it could be perceived as people-pleasing. I did not want to walk up to get prayer so I would not be looked at as attention-seeking or always having something wrong. When I paid no attention to what people thought I would be criticized.

Remember: *But the LORD said unto Samuel, Look not on his countenance, or the height of his stature; because I have refused him: for the LORD seeth not as man seeth; for man looketh on the outward appearance, but the LORD looketh on the heart (1 Samuel 16:7)*

During this season of my life, I was in so much internal pain because of trying to shut down the best parts of myself. I did not want to be a giver anymore because I was giving when I got hurt. Giving love in the way that I love. Through words of encouragement, in service, gifts, and the financial offering. I had dropped down to tithes only which I had never done in all my years of serving the Lord. Subconsciously forming the idea that giving is where I got hurt and if I serve then I may not survive the next blow to my heart. Fear.

Remember we are talking about Loving freely in the context of being yourself. I am talking to the person who has come to regret the way they do things.

I stopped wanting to be me when my actions were mislabeled. What I mean is for a second I did not want to love. Then I had a revelation that I was most free when I gave. I could not control what others saw with their eyes. I remembered their opinion was never my desire. I could control how far I let their words come near my actions. So, I pushed away bitterness; mines and theirs. I pushed away those who tried to help by saying I should stay away. I adjusted to pain and loved through it according to my ability. I could not serve anywhere to a high capacity, but I eased my heart back open for operation. Gratefully this process was quick for me not years. Unfortunately, it also meant it had to come stronger than usual. I had to adjust. When a person breaks their legs, they learn to adjust. As they heal, they learn how much pressure they can and cannot apply to the wound. After enduring this I agree that I am in a better building place than before I was hurt. The reason being I know without a doubt I give love because it is my choice and not for reward. The reward is the bonus, not the requirement. I built a boundary around the why of my identity. You must do the same. The issue was not that I was hurt but it was me trying to shut down the best parts of me to protect myself. Self-preservation freezes you, nothing in and nothing out. You can skip or come out of not loving to protect yourself and instead adjust.

Adjust to what you accept in exchange for your love until you are free of charge. It is better to not be paid at all than to be underpaid and offended. It is better to volunteer than to work for pennies and complain. Accept that you may never be compensated for your worth entirely in an economic deficit of love. If someone pays you heartbreak for your commitment, then raise the requirement. You gave a cow to a person who could only handle you buying them a glass of milk. If you love to bake cookies and you have been criticized about your reason (if your reasons are pure) then BAKE THOSE COOKIES. Come away from those opinions! Opinions from hurt people! Do not repeat those hurt opinions!

A hurt person cannot be the healing for another hurt person unless each sacrifices their whole being for the other. But, let me say that Jesus already died for that. If you are yet to believe Jesus aka Yeshua aka YHWSHI then understand no one is without fault. No one is perfect enough to sacrifice their whole self to be the love that a single person needs. Therefore, you should not try to be or become someone's all and all.

No one is perfect enough to sacrifice their whole self to be the love that a single person needs ...

Repeat after me, "I will not lose me trying not to lose anyone else." Biblically speaking you must lose yourself in your pursuit of freedom. This is what you are doing when you choose to love freely. Beyond whom has hurt you. You are love, how do I know? It is not me who needs to know it. I am already convinced. It is you who must believe it. How can you give what you do not have unless it comes from within you? Have you ever loved anyone, anything, or been loved by anyone or anything? Have you ever operated while in a love deficit? Has your heart ever been broken, and you were still able to do something for someone else? Have you ever cried or been betrayed? If you said yes to two or more of those questions, then know that you are love. If you need more convincing, I recommend reading The Power To Become by Mattie Stanford Johnson. So, what is keeping you from operating? It is the multiple concepts of fear you have attached yourself to and formed a connection with. I was involved off and on with a person for five years. I have known them since 2013. We each played grand roles in the poor state of our relationship. However, the only thing that brought healing after each devastating blow to the heart was love. Me working from my heart produced the healing that I needed for my heart. Often, we think we need the one who hurt us to heal our wound but, you do not turn to cake to lose weight. You address your habits. Our hearts can heal themselves if we allow them to do the work of loving others.

Example: You are 50 pounds above your desired goal. When you go out you talk about how you should do better. You change your diet by coming away from cake for a while. You meet your target and now if you have learned your lesson, when you begin to eat cake again it will be with wisdom. It will be with an inward boundary.

1 Corinthians 13:4-8 (NIV) 4 Love is patient, love is kind. It does not envy, it does not boast, it is not proud. 5 It does not dishonor others, it is not self-seeking, it is not easily angered, it keeps no record of wrongs. 6 Love does not delight in evil but rejoices with the truth. 7 It always protects, always trusts, always hopes, always perseveres. 8 Love never fails. But where there are prophecies, they will cease; where there are tongues, they will be stilled; where there is knowledge, it will pass away.

Introspection Section

What did you learn from this lesson?

_____

_____

_____

_____

_____

_____

As we go deeper into ourselves, we must recall lessons learned. High school geometry utilizes grammar school division.

What round are you on in learning this lesson? Circle it.

1 2 3 4 5 6 7 8 9 10 11 12 13 14 15 16 17 18 19 20 21 22 23 24...

When was the last time you tapped into this lesson?

Lesson Two: Know Your Friends

A friend who believes a lie about you is not a friend to YOU. They are not a friend to who you are now. They do not know you enough to disagree with the lie before asking you about it. Let us say a random stranger came and told you that your best friend hates dogs. Your friend who you have known for 10 years has taken care of 7 rescue puppies. Are you going to believe it? Likewise, can your friends tell you when you are sad, do they ask you when something is wrong? Whether you told the lie to them or they heard it from someone else is the dynamic of your relationship. I do not condone lying but, a good friend or someone who knows you should be able to discern whether you are being truthful or not. Either way, if a friend believes a lie about you then it is no longer you that they are connected with. They are now friends with the made-up version of you. If your friend believes you stole from them, then in their mind they are friends with a thief. Know those who labor among you 1 Thessalonians 5:12. This can be your co-workers, fellow church members, and your friends. Know them!

When I was younger in high school, I hung out with a group of people daily. As I got older, I realized that at that time, no one knew my parents were going through a divorce. I did not know whether my best friend had both of her parents in her life. There was so much time filled with only time itself. I look back and feel that I can sum our friendship in one paragraph. I know I love that friend to this day although we are no longer friends. However, it is hard to know if I ever knew her and vice versa. I believe during our friendship I learned her ways without learning her whys. I understood the way that friend was, but I never questioned the origin. Yet, this was my only platonic friend who did not intervene in my relationships. Whether good or bad, she too understood my ways. When we get to know someone, we have to keep getting to know them.

Sometimes in accepting who a person is we think that is all there is to be accepted about them. Therefore, when people are shocked by the actions of a friend it is hard to move beyond that moment, feeling, or situation. A lot of people I meet and get close to seem to disconnect me from anything before the time I meet them. As if they are my origin. Many do not know that I was born in Chicago after 3 years, spent 10 years in Georgia, and now 13 years again in Chicago. People would fall in love with my ways and not know my middle name, my birthday, or that I even like flowers. Yet, because they love me, they felt I should have the same feeling.

I tried someone at what they said they felt and the more I told of myself the more surprise I heard in their voice and the more judgment they put me under. We are not going to always like what we hear about whom we are getting to know this is where lesson one is also applied.

On the other hand, when you know someone and value all of them regardless of flaw or past you must understand that what you know is not a single file. This person, friend, co-worker, or family member is still Loading. Your job as a friend is not to force this person back into the box according to what you know of them. It is to love them and make sure they are going towards the goals they have set for the better. Their better not the better of your friendship nor what is good in your own eyes. Sometimes it is the friendship that can stop progression, and this is a hard truth you take on in getting to know your friends. Remember: *As iron sharpens iron, so one person sharpens another. Proverbs 27:17*

My birthday has always been pivotal for me. First time I heard my daughter's heartbeat was on my 19th birthday. That same day I was accused of stealing money and although I had never been a thief I was painted as one. I did not know until two years later I was being presented as such but, I had no one who knew me around me at that time. The accusation was that I took the money to get an abortion; the birth of my daughter proved it to be a lie. Those who believed the lies about me were not my friends. This is true in more ways than one. At times when they knew me, we were friends and had friendly moments. Someone to say, "No, Tesia would never do that." You never know the outcome of a situation. Even with all that four years ago whether the story is complete or not I should have known who I was around and likewise. I was young and maybe this was a typical teenage drama. Hopefully, someone finds this book before my age back then and can learn about everyone around them. Because EVERYONE plays a part. You cannot decide if it's important for you to know someone or that they are a small part of your life especially at the beginning of meeting them.

I met a girl once who seemed innocent and young in mind. A few conversations and situations brought us around each other many times. I am oversimplifying the dynamic of the connection but this girl I never considered as an impactful part of my life or even of that time. It is sad to say, although I knew details of her life and we hung out consistently, she was not on my radar as a threat or interest. Here is when lesson two was being developed. I recently found out this same person was at the root of two major situations that took place a few years ago. When we place people in a box and go back to check it, we forget there may be a different person in it then the one we placed in there.

As we are getting to know others, they too are getting to know themselves. Allow your friend the grace to change. Lasting friends are those who evolve while we do. For better or worse we cannot control only our interaction with them. If you're with the same friend for five or six years and all you two do is drink and gossip, then what is it that you know about this friend besides them liking to drink and gossip? Friendships are not proven through traveling or attending events and parties together. I look back at photos taken at different points of my life. At dinners, parties, and personal gatherings I understand that knowing people's ways was never enough.

    I used, to be honest to a fault, now I try to prepare people for the truth. Especially if it is something hard to hear. I have been to at least 13 different schools and 7 different churches. I got my first job at 16 and the sea of people I have come to know is wide. I have grown up in a two-parent home and by the hands of a single mother. I understand walking through the snow with my baby's stroller and having a car seat in the backseat of my foreign car. I understand heartbreak on many levels and healing the same. I have been with and without glasses or contacts and knowing details about a person's life is not knowing that person. When I look back to old photos and videos, I understand it was not meant for me to know what was happening in the background but for me to know each person apart from what was yet to come to my knowledge. As you get to know those around you, you do not allow yourself to become the judge of their life. Apply lesson one and love them as you did before you found out whatever you found out. Read this book as you have been reading this book until you found out I'll turn 24 the day this is published. Knowing who is around you is knowing your friends because you never know who you will need to be a friend to you someday.

Example:

Let's say you have a friend named Sammy and you know that Sammy went looting and brought back 7 diamond necklaces. She brought you some flip-flops she saw you looking at the other day at the beauty supply store. Sammy may be a thief but, it's not about judging your friends, it's about knowing who they are as your friend. Sammy brought those necklaces for her 7 aunties. It is not about judging your friends. It is about knowing that Sammy is not the type to wear jewelry. I do not condone stealing but, hopefully, this example will stick with you.

Luke 10:29-37 (NKJV) 29 But he, wanting to justify himself, said to Jesus, "And who is my neighbor?" 30 Then Jesus answered and said: "A certain man went down from Jerusalem to Jericho, and fell among [b]thieves, who stripped him of his clothing, wounded him, and departed, leaving him half dead. 31 Now by chance a certain priest came down that road. And when he saw him, he passed by on the other side. 32 Likewise a Levite, when he arrived at the place, came and looked, and passed by on the other side. 33 But a certain Samaritan, as he journeyed, came where he was. And when he saw him, he had compassion. 34 So he went to him and bandaged his wounds, pouring on oil and wine; and he set him on his own animal, brought him to an inn, and took care of him. 35 On the next day, [c]when he departed, he took out two denarii, gave them to the innkeeper, and said to him, 'Take care of him; and whatever more you spend, when I come again, I will repay you.' 36 So which of these three do you think was neighbor to him who fell among the thieves?" 37 And he said, "He who showed mercy on him." Then Jesus said to him, "Go and do likewise."

Introspection Section

What did you learn from this lesson?

_____

_____

_____

_____

_____

_____

As we go deeper into ourselves, we must recall lessons learned. High school geometry utilizes grammar school division.

What round are you on in learning this lesson? Circle it.

1 2 3 4 5 6 7 8 9 10 11 12 13 14 15 16 17 18 19 20 21 22 23 24...

When was the last time you tapped into this lesson?

_____

_____

_____

_____

_____

Lesson Three: Accept the Truth Of Others And Prioritize Your Own

Overlapping perspective shapes society's reality. If two people attest to the validity of a thing then it is more credible. However, no experience is the same and each person's life is their own including their feelings. A person can say your actions made them sad, that is their truth. You have the liberty without valid proof to say they are not telling the truth. Unless you heard them say to you or another this particular action in question brought them joy then you cannot truthfully say they should not feel sad or did not feel sad. We must permit people to have their experiences through the lens of their perspectives. We cannot force the glasses by which we see things on to others. We simply offer them in conversation daily.

It is said people are free to feel whatever they want, realistically people feel what they are caused to feel. Think about what brings you joy? If you suffer from depression and joy does not seem to find you then what brings you anxiety? If you are truly free to feel what you want, then pick it right now and hold it for five minutes. Who can come along and tell you that you are not happy, that you are not sad, or frustrated, or anxious? We cannot deny others of their experience regardless of if we interpret them differently. In seeing other perspectives do not deny your own succumbing to someone else's interpretation of your sincere actions. Now, I am speaking to those pure of heart and genuine in their service and giving. The one who encounters suspicion and question of ulterior motive although there be none. Those who do things from their heart. Yes, you can see that your actions made them sad, and you understand why. You may have even gone so far as to connect their childhood trauma to this mishap. BUT if you did not mean for the turnout to be such, then that is your truth.

Do not get so caught up in the story and the how of the other person that you forget that truth of your perspective. This is where phrases like, "I understand how that hurt you. I am sorry my actions made you feel that way. My intentions were not to make you sad but to... I hope you can believe I only wanted to..." come in handy. After you have seen, acknowledged, and understood their position you can then choose to explain yours. It is not your responsibility to make them believe you. The best you can do is hope they understand. Language barriers are not only from country to country, but it is also in the understanding and in the heart. Just because you are speaking the same language does not mean you are being understood as you intend. Overtime your actions and character will show and prove your true intent. Do not stress being misunderstood and that causing offense. Realize that it happens and after trying to clarify let it rest. Meaning stop explaining! It will be what it will be.

    I mentioned before that I was off and on with someone for five years about four years ago. What I did not clarify is that we never officially dated. This is my truth. Around our year three, my senior year I ask after my birthday, because you know that is pivotal for me. I asked her if she wanted to be with me. I had never had to wait on anyone during high school and I was at a point of transition. Ready to date or move on. When I asked, she played and walked away I walked in the other direction. Very dramatic right? Well, she walked over to me and said yes. I planned to ask her out the following day with something sweet attached or whatever. SO, when the following day came I asked her to be my girlfriend and she said no. I was confused as you could imagine. Each time the conversation came up she would get mad. We were in the hallway and her friend walked up and asked, "Are you two together?" I looked at her, I said, "No, I don't know, are we?" She gets mad and says No and that she had to tell me something. What she told me hurt pretty bad but, I walked it off after I cried to my best friend at the time. The next day I tried to approach the conversation and it was the same result. So, I began to move on.

  Spring break was days away and I went on a trip to Canada where our concert choir won 1st place in the international competition against another school. Somewhere in the middle of the night I get a text saying "We've been together for two weekends etc...." I've come to understand what was misunderstood and how it could have been fixed with a simple conversation. I wanted to keep the relationship that I did not know that I was in however, it was a bit too late.

We "broke-up" which still did not seem real to me because the relationship did not exist in my reality. Remaining involved unofficially for two years later we never concluded on who was right during that time. Even to this day six years since those two weeks, years since we have dated. There is still a difference in what we each believed happened. However, I cannot discount her truth because it is not my own. Months before I had a similar experience thinking we were together and were not. Just because you are saying the same words it does not mean you are delivering the same meaning. For a time, I began to apologize for moving on when apparently, we were together. It was okay to acknowledge the feelings of the one I hurt however it was not okay to lose my truth in the process. Repeat after me, "I will not lose me trying not to lose anyone else." My truth is and was that I thought someone wanted to be with me because they said so and when I asked to start a relationship, they would get mad and not tell me why, so I tried to move on to someone who was willing to explain their feelings to me. I now accept that her anger was because she thought we were together, her truth. I thought it was because of rejection. It took me some time to rid myself of feeling rejected and it took some time for her to get beyond it, even those she would mention it from time to time. I could not be impacted by it because I knew my truth. Once we were able to accept each other's truth we were able to move forward. I am not talking about lies.

Accept the truth of others and prioritize your own.

Philippians 2:4-8 (NKJV) 4 Let each of you look out not only for his own interests but also for the interests of others.

Matthew 18:15 (NKJV) 15 Moreover if your brother sins against you, go and tell him his fault between you and him alone. If he hears you, you have gained your brother.

Galatians 6:1 (NKJV) 1 Brethren, if a man is overtaken in any trespass, you who are spiritual restore such a one in a spirit of gentleness, considering yourself lest you also be tempted.

Luke 17:1 (NKJV) 1 Then He said to the disciples, "It is impossible that no offenses should come, but woe to him through whom they do come!

Introspection Section

What did you learn from this lesson?

_____

_____

_____

_____

_____

As we go deeper into ourselves, we must recall lessons learned. High school geometry utilizes grammar school division.

What round are you on in learning this lesson? Circle it.

1 2 3 4 5 6 7 8 9 10 11 12 13 14 15 16 17 18 19 20 21 22 23 24...

When was the last time you tapped into this lesson?

_____

_____

_____

_____

_____

Lesson Four: Apologize

I have made mistakes that hurt others and I have done things on purpose that hurt others. The only thing an apology hurts is pride. Whether you are guilty or not do it genuinely for the sake of peace. Blessed *are* the peacemakers, For they shall be called sons of God. Matthew 5:9 "I'm sorry that hurt you." People like to remove themselves from their own actions when it is convenient. "I'm sorry I hurt you." Sometimes an apology can be seen as an admission of guilt. That is only true for the one who is judging you. Apologies are for when you are sorry and change of action for when you are guilty. An apology given when you are caught is less creditable for this reason.

Apologies are for when you are sorry and change of action for when you are guilty.

Example: Your friend believes your child broke their chair. Without checking you are sure it was not your child. Y'all have an argument. Your friend stops talking to you because the chair was $1400. She finds it was not your child. Her apology would be "I am sorry that I allowed this to come in between our friendship." "I am sorry that I blamed your child." These would be two apologies needed addressing the emotional impact and her own actions. Your apology would be, "I'm sorry I went off during the argument, I became offended by the accusation and I should've checked first."

The only thing an apology kills is pride. An apology does not bring healing directly, therefore sincerity is required. When you give a sincere apology, it causes the pride of the other person to fall. Sure, they may be hurt and deserving of the apology but the things that's holding on to that hurt is pride! Do you remember the effect of self-preservation? Nothing in and nothing out remember? A guard is developed because no apology has ever been given. Have you heard this, "She didn't even say sorry." Or "He didn't even say sorry." This is because in the mind of a victim the least you could do is apologize. What is the voice of pride? "I can't forgive them." "They didn't even apologize." "They don't even care." Oh, and this "She/He not sorry." That last one taps into Lesson 2; we cannot assume we know the feelings of others. I am not saying be obvious what I am saying is don't allow your tainted discernment to fool you! Leaning on tainted discernment is unwise. Tainted by bitterness and pride. Those who are waiting around for an apology to move on. Now perhaps the reason they are upset has not truly surfaced yet, just say sorry according to their hurt.

Do you remember being a child and getting in trouble for being the one who hit back and got caught? So now the adult says to you to apologize and make up even though they do not know what happened. So now you are mad because you feel you shouldn't have had to say sorry?

Well let me say do not be an angry little kid. How many times has Jesus had to take the fall for us? Each wound that is how many times. If you were wrongly accused, you can be upset for a little bit then get over it! You should not in turn wait for an apology for having to apologize. Yes, I am charging you to be a more understanding person! Do not retreat in your own space either, just learn from the incident and do not allow it to alter the way you see yourself. You will then slip into pride and a few worse things like despair. Do not let those spirits or vibes transfer and settle! Give no home for the devil or negative energies within yourself!

What if I am not sorry then what should I apologize for, especially if I did nothing wrong? Ask yourself, do you want this person in your life? Realistically, will this tension affect your everyday life? Why not just get it over? Apologize at least for misunderstanding, then state your true intention and if they receive it then so be it. If they do not accept it then move on from this person and find someone who thinks like you. You are apologizing sincerely; you're not begging for forgiveness.

Matthew 5:23-26 (NKJV) *23 Therefore if you bring your gift to the altar, and there remember that your brother has something against you, 24 leave your gift there before the altar, and go your way. First be reconciled to your brother, and then come and offer your gift. 25 Agree with your adversary quickly, while you are on the way with him, lest your adversary deliver you to the judge, the judge hands you over to the officer, and you are thrown into prison. 26 Assuredly, I say to you, you will by no means get out of there till you have paid the last penny.*

Introspection Section

What did you learn from this lesson?

_____

_____

_____

_____

_____

As we go deeper into ourselves, we must recall lessons learned. High school geometry utilizes grammar school division.

What round are you on in learning this lesson? Circle it.

1 2 3 4 5 6 7 8 9 10 11 12 13 14 15 16 17 18 19 20 21 22 23 24...

When was the last time you tapped into this lesson?

_____

_____

_____

_____

Lesson Five: Trust People to Be Themselves Not Who You Want Them to Be

Expectations sometimes come in subtle ways. Sometimes we do not realize how high our expectation was from reality until we get that reality check called disappointment. Some say expect nothing and what you get will surprise you. NO! That is a statement birthed from a disappointed person. We are coming out of disappointment and bitterness! We are stepping into ourselves! Indirectly, stepping out of and off of others. What do I mean? When was the last time you were shocked by how someone treated you? Have you ever seen that same person treats others like that? You thought because you were you that they would not be them. I know many people who claim trust issues. I trust that a person with trust issues may not trust me. I trust that person will be themself and behave how a person with trust issues will behave until I am shown otherwise. I do not judge this person, holding closely to this one identity for them. I am not shocked when they decide to confide in me, however, I am not disappointed in them or the relationship when they are who they have been. Allow growth for the one you trust dearly.

Sometimes when we meet a person, we trust in their potential rather than their actual. When parents say, "I know my child." It usually means we know what our kid would and would not do behind our backs. Lesson two: Know your friends. Know whomever is around you before you can trust them to be themselves. I am rarely ever surprised by anyone's actions. However, I have been caught off guard twice. You can perceive a surprise by someone's actions by new consistency. "Oh, so Tesia are you saying people can switch up?" YES! That is what I am saying. Also, THAT IS NOT A BAD THING! "Other people's lives are not about us!" Neither do people belong to us... unless you are married but I am not going there. Trust in the LORD with all your heart and lean not on your own understanding; Proverbs 3:5. Stop trying to see people where they will be right now. Hoping for a connection that may grow but overlooking the connect that is current! Think in the right now. I dated a guy and we never saw eye to eye in conversation but for the sake of what might be we kept talking. I thought he was a good guy, and the dates were nice until we would touch on any real topic. He was not a bad guy; however, I am assertive whereas he is more passive aggressive. So, I would address any aggression I felt from him to know the root. He would prefer to laugh it off. You see, in our last conversation I realized I could not rely on him to express what was wrong with him if asked directly. I understood that I could instead trust that how he felt would come out in a form of a joke, good or bad.

"Other people's lives are not about us!"

If you feel that they are on assignment in your life, then that too is not about you! If you have done all that you can to shake a person and here, they are yet and still then stop focusing on them regardless if it feels that they are focusing on you! Let them be them so you can be you. Apply wisdom, not fear.

Psalms 24:1 (KJV) 24 The earth is the Lord's, and the fulness thereof; the world, and they that dwell therein.

Proverbs 3:5-6 (KJV) 5 Trust in the Lord with all thine heart; and lean not unto thine own understanding.

6 In all thy ways acknowledge him, and he shall direct thy paths.

Matthew 13:24-30 (NIV) *24 Jesus told them another parable: "The kingdom of heaven is like a man who sowed good seed in his field. 25 But while everyone was sleeping, his enemy came and sowed weeds among the wheat, and went away. 26 When the wheat sprouted and formed heads, then the weeds also appeared. 27 "The owner's servants came to him and said, 'Sir, didn't you sow good seed in your field? Where then did the weeds come from?' 28 "'An enemy did this,' he replied. "The servants asked him, 'Do you want us to go and pull them up?' 29 "'No,' he answered, 'because while you are pulling the weeds, you may uproot the wheat with them. 30 Let both grow together until the harvest. At that time I will tell the harvesters: First collect the weeds and tie them in bundles to be burned; then gather the wheat and bring it into my barn.'"*

John 13:11 (KJV) *11 For He knew who would betray Him; therefore He said, "You are not all clean."*

John 6:64 (NIV) 64 Yet there are some of you who do not believe." For Jesus had known from the beginning which of them did not believe and who would betray him.

Introspection Section

What did you learn from this lesson?

_____

_____

_____

_____

_____

As we go deeper into ourselves, we must recall lessons learned. High school geometry utilizes grammar school division.

What round are you on in learning this lesson? Circle it.

1 2 3 4 5 6 7 8 9 10 11 12 13 14 15 16 17 18 19 20 21 22 23 24...

When was the last time you tapped into this lesson?

_____

_____

Lesson Six: Do Not Assume They Know

Have you ever been accused of knowing something you had no idea about? Let us say you scuff someone's white Air Force Ones and assume you did it on purpose because you knew where their feet were. How would that make you feel as a person who did not do it on purpose? You would not like it and depending on where you are in your healing you may think about doing it on purpose. Cue lesson One!

Now, stop being the man in the shoes! Do not assume first offenders know your triggers. People who are still learning you do not know all of you. If you are still learning yourself how well should they know you? First offender... show them mercy and walk them through what you feel they should have known. This is your boundary, your feelings, and whatever space they have crossed the line concerning them. We're building boundaries not guards! Put down that offense and allow them to get to know you by informing them just where they hurt you. If the shoes are damaged beyond a simple wipe down, then ask to be reimbursed. Ask them to clean them off, to cover the repair, and offer them the chance to take responsibility. Reasonable responsibility, like admitting they were unaware or saying they will do better. If you receive an apology, then do not look to make them sorry. It is more freeing to cover the incident in love, than to fall into conspiracy theories. Excuse and evaluate your first offenders in that order. After applying Lesson two to your surroundings, you will know rather than assume. Regardless, lean not to your own understanding and if someone oversteps a boundary of yours simply let them know rather than attacking them. It is called a trespass when they've entered your boundary without permission. You have the right to feel however the actions have caused you to feel. Especially if you pray the LORD's prayer "Our father…" Matthew 6:12 And forgive us our debts, as we forgive our debtors. Stop assuming they know they have hurt you. Assuming that they knew what would upset you. Assuming it is even on their mind. When you stop assuming you can then open your mouth and inform them. Then you will know that they know!

Perhaps plenty of times you have given the benefit of doubt to people who transgress after you have told them.

Well, why did you doubt? You will not have to give the benefit of doubt if you have gotten to know them, and you know you have told them before.

It is not about giving the benefit of doubt because we are coming out of that too! It is regardless of your meaning to do what you did. I will not be afraid to state what it is on my mind or on my heart by assuming you already know! You see I feel like people say others already know to get out of the responsibility to address the issues at hand. It is a way to put it in the hands of the other person rather than taking responsibility. So, what if they did do it on purpose? You still have doubt if you must assume. Regardless, confirm the intention first!

Take a moment to see what is going on in their day. "Hey, I know you usually text me 'Good morning' is everything alright?" Remember other people's lives are not about us... unless they are sick in those areas that time does not heal. In this case, they need a pass from you if you have one to give. Remember our hearts can heal it's hurt when we exercise it's love.

This is more about you than it is them. The grace we give comes back to us. You are not pardoning then that they may excuse you in the future! You pardon them because you are operating in lesson One, Loving freely.

Proverbs 14:29 (KJV) He who is slow to wrath has great understanding, But he who is impulsive exalts folly.

Jeremiah 31:3 (KJV) The LORD hath appeared of old unto me, saying, Yea, I have loved thee with an everlasting love: therefore with lovingkindness have I drawn thee.

Psalms 32:1 (KJV) Blessed is he whose transgression is forgiven, whose sin is covered.

Luke 17:3 (KJV) Take heed to yourselves: If thy brother trespass against thee, rebuke him; and if he repent, forgive him.

Introspection Section

What did you learn from this lesson?

_____

_____

_____

_____

_____

_____

As we go deeper into ourselves, we must recall lessons learned. High school geometry utilizes grammar school division.

What round are you on in learning this lesson? Circle it.

1 2 3 4 5 6 7 8 9 10 11 12 13 14 15 16 17 18 19 20 21 22 23 24...

When was the last time you tapped into this lesson?

_____

_____

_____

_____

_____

_____

_____

_____

_____

_____

Lesson Seven: Forgive

Here is a tough one but, it is what you have been building to do. Outwardly, you have excused and pardoned the mistake. You have also asked the offender or trespasser to take responsibility without forcing them to do so! Now, let's deal with those inside feelings. You have tried to let it go but you just cannot seem to. That, "They didn't even say sorry" is starting to come up. God forbid you have told everyone they know, and you know about the offense, gossip, and bitterness just tag-teaming you. People saying let it go but, no one is telling you how to let it go?

Look, forgiveness is a process for your heart primarily. You have been doing some forgiving prior to making it to this part. In actuality, if you've let your heart love freely everyone else except this person then it is your mind that you are at war with. Your mind is building up a wall... A wall sounds good in the aspect of guards and boundaries? No! A wall sits on top of your boundary. It is just an illusion and now people must work harder to get to you both foe AND FRIEND! Sometimes even God! Hear me out... consider your goal here. Are you the ruler of your own land? If so... assuming you said yes, then anyone who walks over the line you can simply walk back across. If you've answered no, then stand up! Do not allow regret, fear of being hurt, pride to protect yourself, and being stabbed by whoever hurt you lock you in!

"Okay Tesia now how do I forgive, where do I start?" You feel betrayal because you felt trust. Be okay with the fact you trusted someone who betrayed you. You were not stupid for trusting them. You were being yourself. Even if trusting others is out of your norm you were being yourself.

1) Forgive yourself.

"It's okay that I trusted, loved, cared for _____ (Insert Name)"

"I know it's hard, but I want to be able to love, care, or trust again."

"When I don't want to love/care, it's because I've been hurt."

"I'm coming out of hurt and into healing."

"I Am myself when I love/care."

"I remember I was not always like this, I used to live in the moment and be free in the moment."

"My goal is not to go back to who I was but to move forward in who I am with the wisdom of who I am."

"I am not broken, I am stronger now than ever, I will become even stronger when I open my heart back up and allow it to heal itself."

"I am in my process where I should be, and I am coming into myself by forgiving myself."

These phrases are phases that will become your truth as you move deeper. Acknowledge and announce where you are and repeat the phrase when you begin to doubt your judgment or shut down. Can I tell you that you are not broken, and you believe me? What you feel is absence of operation! When you go to an amusement park while it is raining, and a ride is not running some may assume it is broken. However, there are just some rides that do not operate in those conditions. You are not broken! You are just not open for operation. Your trust department is closed, and self-preservation hounds are running rampant! You do not know who to trust or who has your back, and everyone looks like an enemy. Well let me tell you they are... wait wait wait do not take that and run with it. They are an enemy of your self-preservation system. They want rust from you, and you trust them back but, that ride is not operating right now.

2) Forgive them for not seeing your pain.

Forgive them for requiring something from you that you could not give. Forgive your family and those closest to you for overlooking your pain. Sometimes others know we are going through something, but they have no idea of how to help us. They barely know how to help themselves. That is not slander, it is a fact. They are probably trying to not let your unforgiveness, suspicion, and mistrust get offend them! You are walking around saying you do not trust a soul, they have a soul that wants to be trusted/loved/cared for, it hurts. This brings me to

3) Change your words, change your perspective.

Put what has happened away from you in time. Use past tense verbs. I have been hurt before but I am better now. I am opening myself up to trusting/loving/caring again. Stop chopping things up to being young and to not knowing better! Change those words. Younger you did the best it could with what it knew and older you will still make mistakes. In 20 years from now will you discount yourself for being young? We will never be old enough to know all that we should know! We will always need to know more. So now….

4) Forgive what you did not know.

Step one of forgiveness should have made this a bit easier to do. In forgiving what you did not know forgive what you will not know! You are too hard on yourself. You expect you to love perfectly and be loved perfectly and to know when someone is not going to love you perfectly. You expect some super knowledge to never get hurt in this battle not healed by time? No, you did not expect perfection. Then why say, you should have known something you did not? Lastly,

5) Love all whom you have forgiven.

What is the point of forgiving if you are just going to be cold towards that person? The forgiveness process is for you and can be done without the presence of the other person. However, if you then encounter the person after you have forgiven them in your own heart why bring it up? Show them love as you show yourself love, you have done well to make it this far, everyone does not need to know it. Now... Start the process again and you will find less hurt in your life and more love given to you than taken from you.

Matthew 18:21-22 (NKJV) 21 Then Peter came to Him and said, "Lord, how often shall my brother sin against me, and I forgive him? Up to seven times?" 22 Jesus said to him, "I do not say to you, up to seven times, but up to seventy times seven.

Introspection Section

What did you learn from this lesson?

_____

_____

_____

_____

_____

_____

As we go deeper into ourselves, we must recall lessons learned. High school geometry utilizes grammar school division.

What round are you on in learning this lesson? Circle it.

1 2 3 4 5 6 7 8 9 10 11 12 13 14 15 16 17 18 19 20 21 22 23 24...

When was the last time you tapped into this lesson?

_____
_____
_____
_____
_____
_____
_____
_____
_____
_____
_____
_____
_____
_____
_____

Lesson Eight: Have Trust and Put It in God

First, I place all my trust in God. Not in myself not in others but I do in fact trust others, however above that I trust God... Okay, now that you have forgiven, hoping you are not reading ahead of your process. This should be a bit easier to consider doing. I am not saying it will be easy.

For this part I want you to get rid of everything you know... except for how to read... For a minute set aside even your name and your birthday. Just be present. That feeling you have is trust. You did not disappear nor did the world cave in or go up in flames. Your body just was as it is. Your body is built to trust, it is your mind that carries doubt.

There was a time I did not trust the seats on the bus. The CTA (Chicago Transit Authority) I had never fallen but my mind had a hard time believing I would not fall. This sounds ridiculous, right? I had ridden the bus for two years and now suddenly, I question why there are no seat belts. It was what if I fell that built distrust. I weighed about 110lbs. I should have had zero worry. Yet, from time to time there I was holding on to my seat. LOL as if holding the sides of my seat would stop the seat from collapsing. I knew logically it made no sense, but logic was not strong enough to convince me. One day I made a choice to just trust it.

In the middle of me trusting I still felt the old feelings of uncertainty while I pushed away the questions of what if and fear. This is a tangible example for what happens in the emotions of a person. Have you ever befriended someone everyone else said you should not? Either you are going to trust the one who told you not to befriend them or you are going to trust yourself and see it through. Trust is like a hole. Either you are going to dig, or you will not. The deeper you dig the deeper the trust is but, now every hole you dig will be deep. The purpose for each hole, for each connection or relationship WILL BE different. You cannot plant a young tree in a hole meant for a seed. Some holes you will give up digging and some land will not allow you to dig at all. Repeat after me, "Your trust and belief go hand and have. You cannot trust something you do not believe. Get your beliefs together! Either you believe you will fall out of that seat or you do not."

It is hard to choose to trust when you do not know what is going to happen. Can I point out that you may never know what will happen so be okay with that. Just be okay with it. Dust off the disappointment and try trusting again, apply wisdom, not fear. Wisdom in trust involves meeting people where they are (before you can do this you must know where they are) that is applying lesson two. Meeting someone where they are is only giving someone what they can handle in your trust. You trusted someone with a secret, they cannot handle secrets. What they can handle is babysitting your child or children. Allow them to show you what they can handle and when you believe they are ready for secrets again then try small not large.

Someone can handle borrowing your car, they bring it back even better than when they left with it. However, they cannot handle showing up for your court date, or being on time. Apply lesson five and leave room for them to be who they are and has been. Perhaps they will surprise you.

Do not allow your past experiences to cause you to doubt your current experience. Allow the previous lesson to help you correctly measure the amount of trust you should give to each person individually. I may meet two people at the same time and trust one with more than the other according to who that person is as a whole. According to who that person has shown me they are combined with how I have seen them be with others. Do not base your relationship off the way you've seen someone treat others and desire that type of connection. You do not know the ins and outs of something you are not in.

    When I became pregnant people tried to convince me that my child's father would be a great father because they saw him post pictures often of his first child. I understood that a photo is not an entire story and they did not know the relationship with him and his daughter. Truly things were not as the photos he posted, and I believe they have come to understand what I knew. Of course, I did not know by experience yet but cause the Lord had caused me to understand it. I remember wondering about where they had placed their trust.

I knew a person who loved people in many ways. I thought it was a good way to be loved. As I got to know this person, I saw everything I overlooked.

Overlooking something does not mean you did not see it. It means you did not look at it. Consider, acknowledge it is there, and name it (know what it is)! You walk into a room and someone asks you what was in the room. You will name what you looked at and you will probably not point out what you looked over. Same with people! You saw the dresser, the bed, the tv, overlooked the clothes on the bed and the paper on the dresser. You say they were caring, giving, and compassionate. You overlooked their aggression, codependency, and lack of consistency.

You trust others and trust yourself in what you see. It may not be seen universally, meaning others may not agree that it is there but, do not exclude how you feel. This goes for people a person is all wrong about too. Perhaps you see redemption when others have seen a hopeless cause, regardless of you must trust something. Why? Because how are you going to be healed where time does not heal if you do not trust?

When you cannot trust men, trust God. God should be the first one you trust but realistically people often make him their last choice. Those who trust him first, should be ready to trust those He use!

Proverbs 3:5 (KJV) 5 Trust in the Lord with all thine heart; and lean not unto thine own understanding. Be careful for nothing; but in every thing by prayer and supplication with thanksgiving let your requests be made known unto God.

Philippians 4:6-7 (KJV) 6 Be careful for nothing; but in every thing by prayer and supplication with thanksgiving let your requests be made known unto God. 7 And the peace of God, which passeth all understanding, shall keep your hearts and minds through Christ Jesus.

Jeremiah 17:7 - 8 (KJV) 7 Be careful for nothing; but in every thing by prayer and supplication with thanksgiving let your requests be made known unto God. 8 Blessed is the man that trusteth in the Lord, and whose hope the Lord is. For he shall be as a tree planted by the waters, and that spreadeth out her roots by the river, and shall not see when heat cometh, but her leaf shall be green; and shall not be careful in the year of drought, neither shall cease from yielding fruit.

No space to write here because you should let it marinate and purchase a notebook. Write what is hard about trusting again and your plan to combat/overcome those hard heart spots.

Lesson Nine: Value Patience and Those Who Are Patient with You

This is not a process or a book for the weak. It is for those who have lived, died, and desire to live again. This is not an overnight process or program. This is a read, do, and be process. Those around you are going to see you squirm as you come back to life. They will feel you require more room to grow, and they will see you drop your guard in becoming operational. They will also see you struggle to be consistent at first try. When you learn to fight a bike, you fall off a few times. You may even resort back to walking until you are ready to try again. That is normal! If you get it first, try without giving up then that Is your experience, and it is also common! Either way, once you have learned to ride a bike, IT IS WITH YOU FOR LIFE!

Those who listen to your cries, pour peroxide, and a bandage on your boo boos ARE IMPORTANT. They too are experiencing your growing pains. They too are impacted by the changes you are going through. The friendship you have outgrown is experiencing lost. Those who let you go even when it is hard and does it with Grace you should be grateful for them. People are not ours. They do not belong to us. We must appreciate the time we have with them. This does not only mean when they leave cause of death but also when they leave because of life! It takes patience and appreciation. Most importantly, it takes acknowledgement of the patience given. Someone heard you mope around, someone encouraged you with a good morning, hello or smile. It may have not been who you wanted it from, it may have been from a stranger or even someone in passing but it came! Say thank you.

Surely as you tried to love freely, some days were harder than others. You love some more than others. It was rough and yet to be perfected. However, people caught the impact of your inconsistency. Say thank you! Show thank you! Be thankful. When you thank others try to thank them the way they like to be thanked. If you've gotten to know them, you know what makes them happy or feel appreciated. Giving a gift card to someone who values thought and effort may not be suitable for that person. If that is how you are a gift card giver then meet them halfway and select it for their favorite restaurant or store. Be grateful for the patience others have. Just because it looks easy does not mean it is, perhaps they began their process 24 years before encountering you and this is the product of it.

Ecclesiastes 7:8 (KJV) 8 Better is the end of a thing than the beginning thereof: and the patient in spirit is better than the proud in spirit.

Matthew 18:20 - 22 (KJV) 20 For where two or three are gathered together in my name, there am I in the midst of them. 21Then came Peter to him, and said, Lord, how often shall my brother sin against me, and I forgive him? till seven times? 22 Jesus saith unto him, I say not unto thee, Until seven times: but, Until seventy times seven

Introspection Section

What did you learn from this lesson?

_____

_____

_____

_____

_____

_____

As we go deeper into ourselves, we must recall lessons learned. High school geometry utilizes grammar school division.

What round are you on in learning this lesson? Circle it.

1 2 3 4 5 6 7 8 9 10 11 12 13 14 15 16 17 18 19 20 21 22 23 24...

When was the last time you tapped into this lesson?

_____

_____

_____

_____

_____

_____

_____

_____

Lesson Ten: Start Again and Keep Going

List the names of the lessons you have read and one main point for each.

_____

_____

_____

_____

_____

_____

_____

_____

_____

_____

_____

_____

_____

_____

_____

Happy You Made It!

Now I can give you the Master Key. My greatest freedom came when I gained my first major revelation of Jesus. Through the following verses.

Philippians 2:9 "Wherefore God also hath highly exalted him, and given him a name which is above every name:"

John 16:23 And in that day ye shall ask me nothing. Verily, verily, I say unto you, Whatsoever ye shall ask the Father in my name, he will give it you.

John 5:46 "For had ye believed Moses, ye would have believed me: for he wrote of me." Says Jesus.

"And the Father himself, which hath sent me, hath borne witness of me. Ye have neither heard his voice at any time, nor seen his shape." John 5:37 KJV

"And God said unto Moses, I AM THAT I AM: and he said, Thus shalt thou say unto the children of Israel, I AM hath sent me unto you." Exodus 3:14 KJV

"Jesus said unto them, Verily, verily, I say unto you, Before Abraham was, I am." John 8:58 KJV

"And God said moreover unto Moses, Thus shalt thou say unto the children of Israel, The Lord God of your fathers, the God of Abraham, the God of Isaac, and the God of Jacob, hath sent me unto you: this is my name for ever, and this is my memorial unto all generations." Exodus 3:15 KJV

"And Moses said unto God, Behold, when I come unto the children of Israel, and shall say unto them, The God of your fathers hath sent me unto you; and they shall say to me, What is his name? what shall I say unto them? And God said unto Moses, I AM THAT I AM: and he said, Thus shalt thou say unto the children of Israel, I AM hath sent me unto you." Exodus 3:13-14 KJV

"And he was clothed with a vesture dipped in blood: and his name is called The Word of God." Revelation 19:13 KJV

"In the beginning was the Word, and the Word was with God, and the Word was God. The same was in the beginning with God." John 1:1-2 KJV

"And they heard the voice of the Lord God walking in the garden in the cool of the day: and Adam and his wife hid themselves *from the presence of the Lord God amongst the trees of the garden." Genesis 3:8 KJV*

"And the Word was made flesh, and dwelt among us, (and we beheld his glory, the glory as of the only begotten of the Father,) full of grace and truth." John 1:14 KJV

"All things were made by him; and without him was not anything made that was made." John 1:3 KJV

"And God said, Let there be light: and there was light." Genesis 1:3 KJV

"The Lord shall fight for you, and ye shall hold your peace." Exodus 14:14 KJV

"[And he was clothed with a vesture dipped in blood: and his name is called The Word of God.] ***And the armies which were in heaven followed him upon white horses, clothed in fine linen, white and clean." Revelation 19:13-14 KJV

"For we wrestle not against flesh and blood, but against principalities, against powers, against the rulers of the darkness of this world, against spiritual wickedness in high places." Ephesians 6:12 KJV

"And he said, Hearken ye, all Judah, and ye inhabitants of Jerusalem, and thou king Jehoshaphat, Thus saith the Lord unto you, Be not afraid nor dismayed by reason of this great multitude; for the battle is not yours, but God's." 2 Chronicles 20:15 KJV

"And he hath on his vesture and on his thigh a name written, KING OF KINGS, AND Lord OF LORDS." Revelation 19:16 KJV

"And I saw heaven opened, and behold a white horse; and he that sat upon him was called Faithful and True, and in righteousness he doth judge and make war."

Revelation 19:11 KJV "

For the Father judgeth no man, but hath committed all judgment unto the Son:" John 5:22 KJV "

His eyes were as a flame of fire, and on his head were many crowns; and he had a name written, that no man knew, but he himself." Revelation 19:12 KJV

Jesus is Yhwh (Yahweh or Yahawah) meaning I AM . I AM in the flesh. The Word of the Father. The Word created us all. Through The Word were we created. Jesus was translated to

English from greek (Iesus). Into Iesus from Hebrew Yahawashi (Yeshua). Call Him as you know Him.

Side Notes

The LORD has been in my life for as long as I can remember. I took interest in Him and He in me at a young age. I devoted my life to Him ten years ago, I rededicated myself six years ago, again three years ago, and now every day. He gave me the desire to write this, the plan and will to get it done. This book is a prophetic word the LORD gave unto me through His Prophet. Of whom I am grateful for His obedience.

To the reader, I hope this has helped bring you into possibility. Thank you for purchasing this book.

To those I have offended I am sorry, I ask that you forgive me, and pardon the inconsistencies I have shown in the learning of these lessons. I am grateful for your forgiveness should you choose to grant it to me.
Thank you, God Bless!

Before You Go

Let me bless you, I pray the mighty works of the Hands of God come forth in your life and be evident to you and those around you. I pray your ways please God so your enemies may be at peace with you. May YHWH, the Word of God bless you through understanding and bless you to understand all languages in your known tongue. May I pray barriers be removed in your heart placed between you and the presence of God. May His light be separated from illusions in your life. I hope you hope again. Praise again, worship in awe and in amazement for God. I pray the Father shows you how to love His son, that they may come unto you. I see you opening your cocoon. First thing I see free and coming out is your right shoulder. Things are coming into color where there was only black and white. Be restored in your senses and allow the Holy Spirit to sweep through the rooms in your heart and in your head. I love you with an uncompromising love. Freely. May the Lord allow you to receive what has been prayed in His timing. Thank you Father, in the mighty name of your son, YaHaWaSHI (Jesus), I pray. Amen

Meet the Author

Tesia Watkins is a Seer Prophet and a single mother of one. She was born in Chicago and spent ten years of her childhood in Georgia. She is President and founder of Profit Together, a 501c3 nonprofit organization. Profit Together, incorporated specializes in community development and operates by campaign through compassion. Out of the chrysalis is her first book. It is also a manifestation of a prophetic word given to her in 2020. To find out more about Profit Together, Incorporated you can visit www.Profittogether.org

www.ingramcontent.com/pod-product-compliance
Lightning Source LLC
Chambersburg PA
CBHW071012160426
43193CB00012B/2020